T0012669

LET'S FILL THIS WORLD WITH KINDNESS

LET'S FILL THIS WORLD WITH KINDNESS

TRUE TALES OF GOODWILL IN ACTION

ALEXANDRA STEWART

JAKE ALEXANDER

CONTENTS

INTRODUCTION

Imagine if an alien from outer space traveled to Earth and tuned into our news channels. What would they see?

They might discover that people come in all shapes and sizes, that some live in strange brick boxes and others move around in snaking lines of colorful wheeled machines. But the alien would also learn some sadder stuff, like the fact our planet is getting warmer and many species are becoming extinct. They might see stories of poor people getting poorer and rich people getting richer, of quarreling countries and bad guys on the run. There would probably be some happier news at the end of the program, but by then the horrified alien might have jammed its spaceship into reverse and zoomed home.

Faced with all this doom and gloom, it would be easy for our alien to believe that Earth is a land that kindness forgot.

But the good news is that's simply not the case. Just look around and you will see countless examples of human kindness in action. Some acts of kindness are very small while others are a little bigger. But all of them, as you'll soon discover, are truly remarkable.

In this book you'll learn about why humankind is naturally kind. It's all in the name! You'll meet ordinary people—grown-ups and children—who helped change our world for the better. They will show you that kindness isn't always gentle. It is sometimes courage, it is often determination, and it is always strength.

Above all, you'll discover that every time you carry out a simple act of kindness—be it a friendly smile or a seat given up to a stranger—you are choosing to make this planet an even better place to live.

So, let's get going and find out how we can fill this world with kindness!

THE SCIENCE OF KINDNESS

How would you describe kindness in a few words? Go ahead, give it a try! It's harder than you think, isn't it? That's because there are many different ways to be kind.

Kindness is being friendly, generous, and considerate to others. It involves sensing and listening to people's needs, as well as caring and trying to help them. It's giving without expecting something in return.

Humans have understood the language of kindness since the dawn of time. In fact, scientists believe that our ability to be kind—not just to our friends and family, but to strangers too—is one of the key reasons we are so successful as a species.

Why? Because it means we are able to work together in big teams (or **societies**)—which has helped us to survive and flourish. We are at our best when we look out for one another, share new ideas, and tackle challenges together.

It's our superpower.

KINDNESS:
THE BEST MEDICINE

So, being kind has helped us succeed as a species. But it also helps each of us in our daily lives. Have you noticed what it feels like when you are kind to somebody?

You might feel a warm glow spread through your body, a lightness in your heart, or an extra spring in your step. That feeling can be explained by science!

Scientists have discovered that when we are kind, our brains release chemicals that have all sorts of wonderful effects on our bodies and our minds.

These smart chemicals—called **neurotransmitters** and **hormones**— improve our mood, make us feel more connected to people, and boost our energy. Incredibly, they can also help us live longer!

It sounds unbelievable—but it's true. Scientists in the U.S. carried out a study on 13,000 adults and found that those who regularly volunteered to help others enjoyed longer, happier, and healthier lives.

THE LOOP
OF KINDNESS

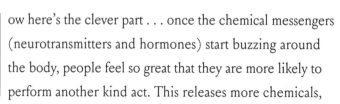

N ow here's the clever part . . . once the chemical messengers (neurotransmitters and hormones) start buzzing around the body, people feel so great that they are more likely to perform another kind act. This releases more chemicals, and so it continues . . . Before they know it, they have created their own loop of kindness!

It's not just the kindness givers who get to ride on the loop. Receiving kindness and even seeing it can trigger the release of kindness chemicals. They are not as strong as those experienced by the giver, but they are just as real. You can probably guess what happens next . . .

Once the chemicals start zipping around the person who has received or seen kindness, they feel motivated to do something kind themselves. The whole cycle starts again!

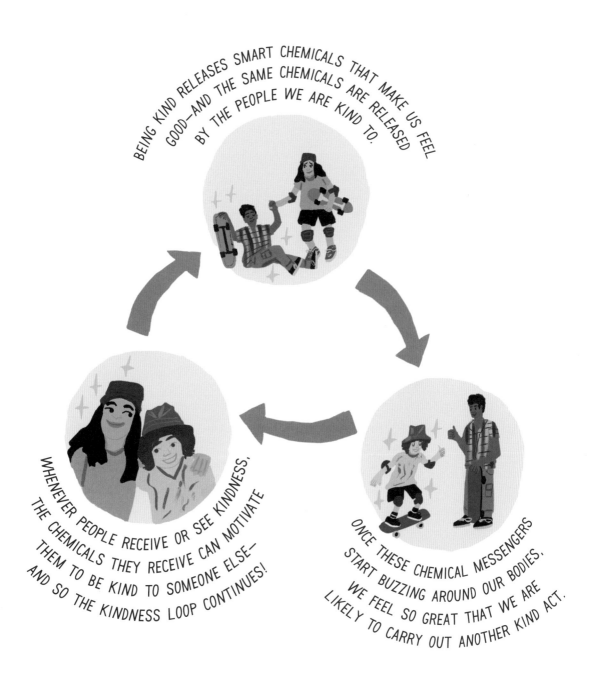

BEING KIND RELEASES SMART CHEMICALS THAT MAKE US FEEL GOOD—AND THE SAME CHEMICALS ARE RELEASED BY THE PEOPLE WE ARE KIND TO.

ONCE THESE CHEMICAL MESSENGERS START BUZZING AROUND OUR BODIES, WE FEEL SO GREAT THAT WE ARE LIKELY TO CARRY OUT ANOTHER KIND ACT.

WHENEVER PEOPLE RECEIVE OR SEE KINDNESS, THE CHEMICALS THEY RECEIVE CAN MOTIVATE THEM TO BE KIND TO SOMEONE ELSE— AND SO THE KINDNESS LOOP CONTINUES!

FLEXING THE KINDNESS MUSCLE

So why can't we just sit back and ride the wave of kindness that is flowing around our world? The trouble is that even though humans have an amazing ability to be kind, we don't always use that ability.

Sometimes we are too busy with our own worries to notice what others are experiencing. Sometimes we're simply not in the mood. Sometimes it's hard to show kindness to someone who isn't being very kind.

Being kind isn't always the easy option! That's why it needs to be worked on. Kindness is like a muscle that needs flexing every day. It needs help to build it up and make it strong. The more you use it, the more powerful it will become.

The people you will read about in the next pages weren't born with bulging kindness muscles! They worked on them too. And they kept going, even when the going got tough.

QUESTIONS

1.

WHY DO YOU THINK IT IS IMPORTANT FOR PEOPLE
TO BE KIND TO ONE ANOTHER?

2.

CAN YOU THINK OF A TIME WHEN YOU HAVE BEEN
KIND TO A FRIEND, A FAMILY MEMBER, OR A STRANGER?
HOW DID IT MAKE YOU FEEL?

3.

CAN YOU THINK OF A WAY TO FLEX YOUR KINDNESS
MUSCLE TODAY?

KINDNESS IN THE FACE OF PERSECUTION

The power of human kindness is often most noticeable when things are at their worst. During these moments—when people are desperate, and lives are in peril—ordinary folk can perform extraordinary deeds.

In this chapter we meet some inspirational humans who risked everything—even their own lives—to help groups of people who had been persecuted. Persecution is the ill-treatment of a group, often because of their ethnicity or religion. They are treated cruelly simply for being who they are.

These remarkable people's stories are a vital reminder that even in the face of cruelty, human kindness remains an unstoppable force.

THE WORLD'S KINDEST VILLAGE

LE CHAMBON-SUR-LIGNON, FRANCE

Nestled among pine forests and pastures in a remote corner of Southeast France lies Le Chambon-sur-Lignon: a small village with a huge heart. It was here, during the dark days of World War II, that a community worked in secret to save the lives of thousands of strangers fleeing persecution.

This story begins in 1940, on a bitterly cold evening in the depths of winter. Busy with household chores, Magda Trocmé—the wife of Le Chambon's pastor, André Trocmé—was interrupted by a mysterious knocking on her front door. Waiting outside stood a woman with her shoulders hunched against the night air. Her flimsy shoes were soaking, and she was shivering with cold and sheer terror. Magda ushered her into the warmth and soon discovered that the woman was Jewish and on the run, in fear for her life.

At that time in France, thousands of Jewish people, including children, were being hunted down and sent to prison camps, to await certain death. In June of that year, Nazi Germany had conquered France and begun a campaign of terror against Jewish people. They also targeted Roma and Sinti people, gay people, physically and mentally disabled people, Black people, and many others. The woman now sitting by Magda's fireplace had just narrowly escaped the Nazis.

Horrified by what was unfolding around them, Magda and André called on the local villagers to join their daring rescue mission. Although protecting Jews was punishable by death, the folk of Le Chambon opened up their homes, schools, hotels, and hiding places. They discovered that many of the people who were seeking shelter were children who had been separated from their parents. The villagers forged new identification cards for their top-secret guests. They fed and clothed them and taught the younger ones in their schools.

It was not long before the villagers' kindness spread—from person to person, farm to farm, and village to village. Soon a wide area around Le Chambon was involved in the rescue effort. As word of the neighborhood's work traveled, more and more refugees arrived on their doorsteps. Not just Jewish people—but anyone in need.

Together, the residents of Le Chambon and other nearby villages quietly and courageously saved the lives of more than 5,000 people.

One of those 5,000, a young boy called Eric Schwam, never forgot their kindness. Nearly eighty years later, Eric left a huge sum of money to the entire village when he passed away. His only wish was that it should be spent on improving the lives of the village's young people.

Today, a memorial stands proudly in Le Chambon, dedicated to the infectious spirit of kindness that saved so many lives. The villagers continue to offer shelter to refugees and migrants from around the world. Together, they ensure that the beacon of kindness lit by their ancestors continues to burn brightly.

THE UNDERGROUND RAILROAD

HARRIET TUBMAN, UNITED STATES

Harriet Tubman was born into slavery in Maryland in the 1820s. Because she was Black, Harriet was not allowed to be a citizen of the U.S., which meant she didn't have the government-granted rights or protections that other people did. Because of where she was born—south of the imaginary line that divided the country into states where slavery was illegal (the North) and legal (the South)—she was considered to be owned by the people whose property she lived and worked on.

Harriet made the long and dangerous journey to freedom in 1849, along something called the **Underground Railroad**. This was not an actual railroad track but an illegal system of secret routes and safe houses used by enslaved people fleeing to the North. The railroad was run by men and women who were all fierce opponents of slavery. While some provided shelter and food to the "passengers," others, called "conductors," guided them along the way.

Harriet managed to complete her journey, but she soon decided to use her **liberty** to help others gain theirs. Risking everything, she headed back south, where she became the first female conductor on the Underground Railroad.

Harriet returned to Maryland at least thirteen times, leading around seventy enslaved people to safety—including her own friends and family. Every time Harriet did this, she faced the very real chance of being seized by armed "slave hunters." Had they caught her, they would have shown no mercy. Despite this, Harriet never lost her nerve and never lost a passenger.

In 1861, the American **Civil War** broke out between the South (the **Confederacy**), which was in favor of slavery, and the North (the **Union**),

which was against slavery. Harriet joined the fight. Over the next four years she served in the Union Army as a cook, laundress, spy, and nurse, tending to wounded soldiers and fugitives who had escaped from slavery. She also led Union soldiers during a daring raid in South Carolina, freeing around 750 enslaved people.

We can only imagine Harriet's overwhelming joy when the U.S. government officially abolished slavery in 1865! After a long and eventful life, Harriet died of pneumonia in her home in Auburn, New York, in 1913. Yet her bold and fearless kindness continues to touch people's lives. Today, her story continues to be told in countries around the globe—inspiring young and old to follow her lead in making the world a better place for all.

FIGHTING APARTHEID

ADELAINE AND WALTER HAIN, SOUTH AFRICA

Adelaine and Walter Hain were born in 1920s South Africa to white English-speaking families. "Wal" and "Ad" both enjoyed happy childhoods, yet beyond the gates of their comfortable homes lay a far bleaker world. It was a world in which Black South Africans and other South African people of color were denied the same freedoms and rights as white South Africans—even though the white South Africans were in the **minority**. Under laws passed by the country's white rulers, Black people were not allowed to do many things, like vote, travel freely, apply for certain jobs, or even live where they wanted.

The situation grew even worse in 1948 when the government introduced a system of **apartheid**—a word from the Afrikaans language meaning "apartness." Hundreds of new racial laws were enforced. People who disobeyed the rules were arrested, imprisoned, and even killed.

Black South Africans put up a fierce resistance to the brutal regime. This fight for freedom was led by a political party called the African National Congress (ANC). One of its organizers was a young Black lawyer named Nelson Mandela, who would become a leading figure in the fight against apartheid.

Horrifyingly, most white South Africans supported apartheid, while only a small number were appalled by it. Among this number were Wal and Ad. Unwilling to watch those around them suffer, they decided to take a stand. The pair threw themselves into supporting the dangerous work of anti-apartheid **activists**.

Wal and Ad hosted political meetings in their home, sheltered people on the run, visited prisoners, and sent food packages to the prisoners' families. While Wal was at work at his architectural firm, Ad traveled to the city's law courts, offering support to the defendants. One fifteen-year-old boy, who many years later became an important judge, remembers Ad bringing him a bar of chocolate on each day of his trial. It was the first time he had ever received kindness from a white person.

When Nelson Mandela was arrested and sent to court for his anti-apartheid activity in 1962, Ad went along each day to support him. She was often the only person in the courtroom's "whites only" gallery. Each morning, as he arrived in the dock, Nelson saluted her with a clenched fist—a gesture she returned in **solidarity**.

Ad and Wal's activities got them into a lot of trouble. On one occasion they were arrested and imprisoned for two weeks. They were banned from political activity, forbidden from meeting more than one person at a time, and couldn't even enter their children's school. Eventually, in 1966 they had to leave the country for good, after the government banned local companies from employing Wal.

Finally, in 1990—after twenty-seven grueling years as a political prisoner—Nelson Mandela walked free from jail. Four years later, he was elected president of South Africa. This historic moment marked the official end of apartheid. It was the first time people of all races had voted in a national **election** in South Africa.

Nelson Mandela came to be one of the most celebrated figures in the world. Yet, despite his fame, he never forgot the kindness Ad and Wal had shown him and his fellow activists. In 2000, while seventy-three-year-old Ad was recovering in the hospital from a bad fall, she received an unexpected telephone call. "Hello, Mandela from South Africa here," said the cheerful voice. "Do you remember me?"

QUESTIONS

1.

HOW DID THE KINDNESS OF STRANGERS HELP THE REFUGEES ARRIVING IN LE CHAMBON-SUR-LIGNON?

2.

WHAT DO YOU THINK HARRIET TUBMAN WAS THINKING WHEN SHE DECIDED TO TRAVEL BACK SOUTH ALONG THE UNDERGROUND RAILROAD TO HELP OTHER ENSLAVED PEOPLE FIND FREEDOM?

3.

WHY DO YOU THINK AD AND WAL CONTINUED TO SUPPORT BLACK SOUTH AFRICANS DURING APARTHEID EVEN THOUGH THEY GOT IN TROUBLE FOR DOING SO?

KINDNESS IN THE FACE OF PREJUDICE

The world contains people of beautiful variety. People with different faiths, interests, skin colors, loves, languages, styles, and, of course, personalities. It's what makes the world such a rich and wonderful place!

Some people don't understand this. These people might judge or even hate others for no reason at all, except that they are not like them. This is called prejudice.

The people we are about to meet each took a brave stand against prejudice. Instead of returning hate for hate, they chose to respond with patience and goodness.

FIGHTING FOR LGBTQ+ RIGHTS

MAGNUS HIRSCHFELD, GERMANY

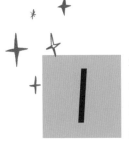

In the year 1906, Germany was gripped by a royal scandal. A national newspaper published an article about a German prince having a love affair with a German army General. The story was explosive because, at that time, love between men was illegal.

Outraged by this **libelous** attack on his character, the General took the article's author to court. But as the trial unfolded, one of the experts who was called to give evidence caused even more shock. This expert was Dr. Magnus Hirschfeld.

Magnus told the court that love between two men was as pure and as natural as love between a man and a woman. He explained that people should not be punished for their **gender** or for their **sexuality**. Gender describes how someone identifies, whether they are a boy, a girl, or **non-binary**, for example. Sexuality describes who someone is attracted to—some people are attracted to people whose genders are different from their own, others are attracted to people who are the same gender as them, and some people are attracted to both, or neither.

Magnus bravely stood up for what he knew was right and explained to the court that people choose neither sexuality nor gender—it's part of who they are.

His words caused a wave of outrage because most people at that time did not understand this. Despite the anger, Magnus was determined to change people's views. He made it his life's work to fight for people's right to love whoever they wanted.

Starting back in 1897, he had helped set up the Scientific-Humanitarian Committee—the world's first gay rights movement, which pushed to end Germany's anti-gay laws. The committee aimed to teach the public about sexuality and gender and encouraged LGBTQ+ people to stand up for their rights.

In 1919 Magnus opened the Institute for Sexual Science in Berlin. The Institute offered medical care, research opportunities, and counseling. It was the first of its kind in the world. Magnus offered support and advice to people in same-sex relationships, and he also helped **trans** people. Society expected that certain people would identify as certain genders because of the bodies they were born with, but for Magnus's trans patients, neither society's expectations nor the bodies they were born in determined their gender. The Institute was a groundbreaking medical institution, and also a community center where people could come together in the library, at parties, or simply give everyday support to each other.

Yet there were still those who were angered by Magnus's work. In 1921, he was beaten up by a stranger who did not agree with his views.

The rise of the Nazi Party made life even more dangerous as Magnus was gay and Jewish. Threats cast a dark shadow over his freedom and safety. In 1933, Nazi thugs ransacked his institute and burned all of the precious books and research papers in its library. Luckily, Magnus was in Paris at the time, but he would never return to Germany. He died two years later.

After his death, Magnus's trailblazing ideas and fierce determination continued to light and lead the way in the study of sexuality and gender. He is now recognized as a courageous pioneer of one of the first movements for LGBTQ+ rights.

"Soon the day will come," he wrote, "when science will win victory over error, justice a victory over injustice, and human love a victory over human hatred and ignorance."

DESIGNING A WORLD FOR EVERYONE

SINÉAD BURKE, IRELAND

inéad Burke is a disability activist who has spent her life campaigning for kindness. The success of her work has seen her celebrated on the cover of the world's most famous fashion magazine, *Vogue*, and has led her to meet with countless important people—from pop stars and presidents to prime ministers and princes. Sinéad was born with **achondroplasia**. This **genetic condition** means she has shorter-than-average limbs—as a **little person**, she is just over three feet tall.

ACHONDROPLASIA.

Even at age eleven, Sinéad understood the importance of talking about what it means to be a little person. On her first day of school, she marched to the front of the class and spelled out achondroplasia for her classmates to help them learn and understand.

When Sinéad was a fashion-loving teenager, she was not able to buy the things she wanted to. Fashionable clothes and shoes were not designed to fit Sinéad's body shape. She often had her outfits adjusted by a tailor. She was frustrated by clothing stores, where rails were usually too high for her to reach.

But Sinéad was determined to make her voice heard, so she began to write about the fashion industry on her **blog**. She talked about how the fashion and design worlds did not think about the needs of disabled people, and why that needed to change.

Over time, people began paying attention. She was invited to the White House to speak about fashion and disability. Major fashion designers across the world took notice of what she was saying. They designed dresses especially for her and she became the first little person to attend the Met Ball (a famous party held each year in New York to celebrate fashion)! Even more importantly, designers started to think about—and design for—the wider community of little people.

But, although Sinéad has tackled the tough task of getting big businesses to change the way they design things, a harder task remains: to change some people's attitudes toward disabled people.

Even as an adult, she experienced bullying. When a schoolboy leapfrogged over her head in a street in Dublin, while his friend filmed it, Sinéad hatched a plan to tackle this sort of unkindness head on.

She visited schools across Dublin to speak with pupils about her experiences as a little person. She encouraged their curiosity and questioned their thinking. She challenged them to choose kindness and understanding over prejudice. "I didn't choose to be in this body," she told them. "But how we behave to ourselves, and other people, is a choice."

Sinéad strongly believes that we all have a part to play in making the world a safer, kinder, and more **inclusive** place for everyone. Disability campaigners cannot do it alone, she says. "We need you all to stand with us."

COMBATING HATRED AND THE KKK

DARYL DAVIS, UNITED STATES

When Daryl Davis was ten years old, he took part in a Cub Scout parade in his hometown of Belmont, Massachusetts. As he was marching proudly along, a small group of onlookers began to pelt him with bottles, rocks, and garbage.

Daryl didn't understand why they were doing it. He wondered if they had something against the Scouts. It was only when he got home that his parents sat him down and explained racism to him: he had been attacked because he was Black.

Daryl was baffled. He couldn't understand why people would want to hurt him because of the color of his skin. "How," he wondered, "can you hate me when you don't even know me?" It was a question he would dedicate his life to answering.

Daryl was a talented musician and grew up to become a professional pianist, entertaining audiences around America. One night, in 1983, he went and played with a band in a town called Frederick, in the Southern state of Maryland. He was the only Black person in the room.

When Daryl had finished playing, a man from the audience congratulated him on his skilled performance and offered to buy him a drink. The man confessed it was the first time he had ever had a drink with a Black person. When Daryl asked him why, the man admitted he was a member of the Ku Klux Klan.

The Ku Klux Klan (KKK) is the oldest hate group in America, with a long history of violence. The KKK's target has typically been Black Americans, but it has also attacked Jews, immigrants, LGBTQ+ people, and Catholics.

Instead of walking away in disgust, Daryl decided to stay and talk to the man. Choosing to position kindness against hatred, he listened patiently to what the man had to say. By the end of the evening, the pair had exchanged telephone numbers and gradually, bit by bit, they became friends.

This extraordinary encounter led to further meetings between Daryl and other members of the KKK. Daryl would share meals with them, welcome them into his home, and talk with them for many hours. He gently questioned their beliefs and politely challenged them. He even attended KKK rallies.

What Daryl was doing was dangerous, and there were times when he feared for his life. Nevertheless, his patience and kindness didn't falter. By extending the hand of friendship to people who should have been his worst enemies, he succeeded in dissolving their prejudice. What's more, his kindness inspired them to treat others better.

Many of Daryl's KKK friends left the organization because they no longer believed in its ideas. Thanks to Daryl, they realized that kindness felt so much better than hate.

Today, Daryl works hard to spread his message about the power of kindness. "No matter how hard it is, it's worth being kind," he says. "When we return hate with hate, frustration with frustration, unkindness with unkindness, it creates a toxic cycle. But when we return negativity with kindness, we help teach others to be kind. We have the opportunity to break the cycle."

QUESTIONS

1.

HOW DID MAGNUS HIRSCHFELD USE HIS SCIENTIFIC
KNOWLEDGE TO ENCOURAGE PEOPLE TO BE KIND TO OTHERS?

2.

DARYL DAVIS HAS SPENT MANY YEARS MEETING AND TALKING
TO MEMBERS OF THE KU KLUX KLAN. WHAT EMOTIONS DO
YOU THINK HE FELT DURING THESE CONVERSATIONS?

3.

CAN YOU THINK OF ANY WAYS IN WHICH WE CAN
ALL STAND AGAINST PREJUDICE USING KINDNESS?

KINDNESS IN WAR

War is a time of terrible fear, sadness, and dread. When destruction is all around, kindness can seem very far away. Yet as our previous stories have shown, brave people can find it within themselves to tackle the scariest situations with **compassion**.

Wherever you are, look closely at the world and you will soon find kindness at work—sometimes in the most unlikely places and often with the most extraordinary results.

FRIENDSHIP IN THE CLOUDS

CHARLIE BROWN AND FRANZ STIGLER, GERMANY

The American B-17 bomber plane had been ferociously pounded by enemy aircraft. With two of its engines faltering, half its tail missing, and its systems failing, it was a miracle it was still flying. Even worse, the brave **tail gunner**, Sergeant Hugh "Ecky" Eckenrode, had been killed and most of the men on board were badly injured.

It was December 1943. Four years since the start of World War II, five days before Christmas and a few hours into the American crew's first ever bombing mission over Germany. They suspected it would also be their last.

As the plane limped back toward its base in the United Kingdom, the pilot, Second Lieutenant Charlie Brown, looked out of his window. There, flying menacingly alongside him, was a German fighter aircraft, the Messerschmitt Bf 109.

Charlie closed his eyes and shook his head. When he opened them again, the aircraft was still there. Bracing himself for what would surely be the end, Charlie was astounded when it didn't come.

Incredibly, rather than attacking them, the German pilot signaled for Charlie to land and surrender. Charlie decided to ignore the request and continue on his flightpath. All the while, the German aircraft remained by the B-17's side.

Eventually, after safely escorting them out of German territory, the pilot saluted, peeled away, and vanished. Stunned, and relieved, Charlie made it back to England with the remaining eight members of his crew, safe and sound.

Unsurprisingly, Charlie never forgot the mystery German pilot. He knew that if the pilot had been caught helping him, he could have been executed for **treason**.

Decades later, he remained so thankful that he decided to try and find his unlikely guardian angel. In 1990, he succeeded! The pilot's name was Franz Stigler and, during the war, he had been one of Germany's most talented fighter pilots. When the two men finally met, Franz explained why he had helped Charlie all those years ago.

Looking into the smashed windows of the B-17 bomber, he had not seen the enemy but fellow humans in need. "To me it would have been the same as shooting at a parachute," Franz said. "I just couldn't do it. I just hoped that he would bring his wounded men home."

Charlie and Franz remained the best of friends until their deaths—just a few months apart, in 2008.

THE RED CROSS

HENRI DUNANT, SWITZERLAND

In June 1859, a young Swiss merchant called Henri Dunant traveled to the village of Solferino in Northern Italy. Something of an **optimist**, he was hoping to have a business meeting with the French ruler, Napoleon III, who was involved in a bloody battle with the Austrians in the area.

By the time Henri arrived in the village, the fighting had ended—but the devastation was not over. Thousands of dead soldiers lay across the battlefield. Meanwhile, many more were injured and dying, with nobody to treat them.

A horrified Henri immediately forgot his business meeting and set about organizing help for the wounded. Working with the villagers, he set up a makeshift hospital in a church, where soldiers from both sides received care.

When Henri returned to his hometown of Geneva, Switzerland, he could not forget the terrible things he had seen. Determined to stop such suffering from happening in future wars, he wrote about what he had experienced in a book called *A Memory of Solferino*.

Henri's book set out a revolutionary new idea! It proposed that every country should come together to create a **neutral** and independent organization of volunteers. These volunteers would protect the wounded and suffering in times of war, no matter what side they were on.

Henri shared his book with many leaders throughout Europe and was thrilled by their enthusiastic response. His idea resulted in the creation of the International Red Cross and Red Crescent movement—the world's largest **humanitarian** network.

Today, the Red Cross and Red Crescent movement operates around
the globe, providing emergency relief and lifesaving help to people affected
by war and natural disaster.

But Henri's achievement did not end there. His idea also led to the first
Geneva Convention—a set of rules governing how nations at war should
behave. The twelve countries that signed up to the rules promised that, when
at war, their armies would care for wounded soldiers, whatever side they were
on. They also promised not to attack medics or **civilians** who were helping sick
or wounded soldiers. Over the years, more rules have been added and more
countries have signed up to them. Today, 196 countries around the world
have agreed to follow the Geneva Conventions.

THE ORPHANS OF SIRET

SIRET, ROMANIA

The small town of Siret used to be known for its orphanage, where thousands of children were once hidden from sight. Among them were Lenuta Gavriluta and Rodica Marginean. At that time, Romania was ruled by a **dictator**, Nicolae Ceaușescu, who was responsible for the terrible conditions at the orphanage.

This heartbreaking story only came to light when Ceaușescu was toppled from power in 1989. Soon afterward, aid workers from around the world traveled to Siret to help the children.

In the years that followed, the orphans of Siret tried to rebuild their lives. Many who stayed in the town, including Lenuta and Rodica, now live in homes provided by the School for Life Foundation—a charity that gives former Romanian orphans the help they need to live a comfortable life.

But Lenuta and Rodica's story does not end there. The small town of Siret sits on Romania's border with Ukraine. In 2022, shortly after Russia's president, Vladmir Putin, ordered the invasion of Ukraine, thousands of refugees began pouring into Siret. They were cold and terrified. They had left their homes behind and needed a safe place to go.

Filled with compassion, Lenuta and Rodica decided to help. Despite owning very little themselves, they wanted to share whatever they had.

They welcomed refugees into their home, fed them, and supported them. They even gave up their own beds to make their guests more comfortable. They bought the children sweets and made one seven-year-old boy a birthday cake.

Lenuta and Rodica's childhoods had been difficult in the orphanage. So, even though they grew up without affection, laughter, and birthdays, they were determined that no child should suffer as they did.

"The little ones are frightened, affected by the war," Lenuta explained. "I understand. I lived through my own war and now I want to help others fleeing theirs . . . It's good to help."

QUESTIONS

1.

WHY DO YOU THINK CHARLIE BROWN WANTED TO SEARCH FOR
THE MYSTERY GERMAN PILOT ALL THOSE YEARS LATER?

2.

HOW DID THE KINDNESS OF HENRI DUNANT LEAD TO THE
CREATION OF THE INTERNATIONAL RED CROSS AND RED
CRESCENT MOVEMENT?

3.

CAN YOU FIND THE EXAMPLE OF A KINDNESS LOOP IN THE
STORY OF THE ORPHANS OF SIRET? SEE IF YOU CAN EXPLAIN
HOW KINDNESS CAN BE PASSED ON TO OTHERS.

KINDNESS IN THE FACE OF DISASTER

Throughout the previous chapters, we have seen how kindness can triumph in the face of **injustice**. In the next stories, we meet people who went out of their way to help total strangers when disaster struck.

When earth-shattering events occur, we realize we are all on the same side. By working together in these moments of disaster, humans can come out stronger than ever!

These are just three examples from history, but I wonder if you can think of others that have happened near you in more recent times?

TITANIC SELFLESSNESS

HAROLD LOWE, UNITED KINGDOM,
AND THE PASSENGERS AND CREW ON THE RMS TITANIC

As the world's largest ship sank beneath the icy Atlantic waters, shivering survivors watched, helplessly and in horror.

It was 2:20 a.m. on April 15th 1912. Less than three hours earlier, the mighty RMS Titanic had been making excellent speed on her first voyage from Europe to New York. But progress quickly turned to disaster when the ship crashed into a lurking iceberg, fatally puncturing the **hull**.

As the ship's mass of steel and iron began to sink beneath the waves, it became clear that not everyone could be saved. There were only enough lifeboats for half of the 2,200 people aboard. In the end, just 706 people lived to tell the terrible tale.

In the weeks after the sinking, investigators and newspapers gathered stories to understand how the tragedy had struck. While reporting, they discovered acts of incredible generosity and kindness.

One of the Titanic's most celebrated heroes was Harold Lowe, the ship's fifth officer. Harold commanded the only lifeboat to return to where the ship had disappeared. He searched for survivors in the dark and freezing water. He pulled four people out before rowing to the rescue of another lifeboat that was about to sink.

Harold was not alone in his selflessness. People handed their lifejackets to strangers, and others gave up their seats on lifeboats. Lost and terrified groups of passengers were led through the maze of sinking corridors and stairs to the waiting lifeboats above. Adults looked after children that were not their own, and others kept spirits up by encouraging people to row and sing.

In the heart of the vessel, engineers and firemen stayed at their stations, keeping the water pumps and electricity going. Although they knew they would go down with the ship, they were intent on keeping the Titanic afloat and lit for as long as possible so that others could escape.

Weeks later, as an official inquiry examined the failures that had caused the disaster, stories like these provided glimmers of light and healing. These amazing tales of selflessness and kindness show that, even in the face of disaster, humanity can shine.

THE TOWN THAT HOSTED THOUSANDS

GANDER, NEWFOUNDLAND, CANADA

On September 11th 2001, the small town of Gander in Newfoundland, Canada, received some unexpected guests—thirty-eight aircraft carrying around 7,000 people.

A short while earlier, horror had unfolded in the skies over America. In a series of carefully planned attacks, terrorists had hijacked and crashed four planes. A total of 2,977 people from ninety-three nations were killed.

Soon after the attacks, the U.S. closed its airspace and hundreds of planes in mid-flight were diverted to Canadian airports. Thirty-eight of these went to Gander International Airport. Everyone onboard was going to need a place to stay.

Just 10,000 people lived in Gander, and the town had a tiny amount of hotel space—not enough for its 7,000 visitors! So the locals came to the rescue. Tired, hungry, and upset passengers were greeted with warm smiles, hot meals, beds, and showers. Schools and churches were turned into dormitories, while some people put passengers up in their own homes.

Households donated piles of shampoo, soap, clothing, and food to the visitors. The locals even put on entertainment for their guests—including bowling matches and concerts by local bands.

The passengers were deeply grateful for the kindness they received, yet their hosts did not believe they had done anything out of the ordinary. "You don't turn your backs on people in need," said one.

The passengers, in turn, never forgot the kindness they had received. Those aboard one flight collected money for a scholarship fund for students in the Gander area. Others, who had stayed in Gander's neighboring town of Appleton, donated $5,000 to their hosts. Appleton used it to build a Peace Park.

Each year, Appleton holds a ceremony to honor those killed on 9/11, and to show appreciation for the people who cared for the stranded passengers. "There is goodness in the world," said Appleton's Mayor in 2017, "that floats to the top in times of disaster."

THE GREAT EAST JAPAN EARTHQUAKE

FUKUSHIMA, JAPAN

On March 11th 2011, a colossal earthquake struck off the northeast coast of Japan. Less than an hour after the earthquake, the first of many **tsunami** waves hit Japan's coastline. The waves—some the height of a twelve-story building—swept inland, wiping entire towns off the map.

It was a terrible natural disaster, but worse was to come. At the Fukushima Daiichi Nuclear Power Plant, 155 miles north of Tokyo, waves crashed over defenses and flooded the reactors, sparking a major disaster. With hazardous **radiation** leaking into the atmosphere, tens of thousands of people were forced to evacuate their homes.

Together, the earthquake, tsunami, and nuclear meltdown resulted in thousands of deaths and the evacuation of half a million people.

While the victims were still in shock, help was on its way. Money, goods, and around 1.4 million volunteers poured into the area. The volunteers set up shelters and community kitchens for survivors.

Some handed out food, clothes, and blankets. Acrobats even came to entertain the children.

Meanwhile, at the damaged nuclear power plant, employees battled to prevent the disaster from getting worse. They did so despite knowing that they were exposing themselves to extreme levels of radiation.

One of them, a father of two children, Atsufumi Yoshizawa later explained: "No one was forced to stay . . . but we knew that we were the only people capable of saving the plant."

The compassion that lit up those dark days remains an inspiration to the people of Japan. On the ninth anniversary of the disaster, Uchibori Masao, Governor of the Fukushima region, told the world:

"We have been supported by a lot of kindness . . . This has strengthened our desire to do the same for others. Through these experiences we have realized the power of kindness."

QUESTIONS

1.

CAN YOU EXPLAIN HOW THE LOCAL PEOPLE LIVING IN GANDER SHOWED KINDNESS TO THE PASSENGERS ON THE PLANES THAT LANDED THERE? AND HOW DID THE PASSENGERS SHOW KINDNESS TO THE PEOPLE OF GANDER AND APPLETON?

2.

HOW DO YOU THINK THE WORKERS FELT AS THEY ARRIVED TO HELP AT THE NUCLEAR PLANT IN FUKUSHIMA AFTER THE DISASTER? WHAT ABOUT THE OTHER VOLUNTEERS WHO CAME TO THE AREA TO HELP?

3.

CAN YOU THINK OF ANY EXAMPLES YOU MAY HAVE SEEN WHERE PEOPLE HAVE BEEN KIND TO OTHERS IN THE FACE OF DISASTER?

KINDNESS IN THE FACE OF ILLNESS

We've all been unwell at one point or another. It could be a sore throat, a horrible bug, or something more serious. Do you remember how you felt the last time you were sick? Maybe you were tired, or groggy, or didn't feel like yourself?

When that happens, we need the care of the people around us. When we feel that someone is looking out for us, it can actually help us get better more quickly!

As our next stories will show, you don't have to be a medic or a pharmacist to help in these moments. Sometimes, the treatment we appreciate the most is a simple dose of human kindness.

EMPATHY TRIUMPHING OVER FEAR

GAY MEN'S HEALTH CRISIS, UNITED STATES, AND PRINCESS DIANA, UNITED KINGDOM

Our story begins in the early 1980s, when a mysterious new virus was sweeping the world. Doctors gave it the name Human Immunodeficiency Virus (HIV) because it attacks the body's immune system—the system that helps us fight off infections and diseases.

Back then, most people who caught HIV went on to develop AIDS, a deadly collection of infections that take over when HIV has weakened the body.

As the number of infections quickly rose around the world, panic began to spread. People were terrified of what was happening, and they had lots of questions: Where had HIV come from? What exactly was it? How did it spread?

One thing that was clear at the time was that gay communities had been hit hard by the virus. Because of all the unanswered questions, rumors ran wild. Many people wrongly believed they could catch HIV simply by shaking the hand of someone with the virus.

This fear led to many scared and lonely HIV patients hiding their illness. People who were sick were often not given sympathy—even by their own family and friends.

Shocked by this terrible behavior toward sick people, members of gay and lesbian communities decided to act. One of these groups, Gay Men's Health Crisis (GMHC), set up the world's first AIDS hotline, where people could call for help and advice. They introduced "buddy" systems—where volunteers took people to the hospital and visited those who were dying from AIDS. Whether it was doing the shopping or simply giving them a hug, the volunteers let their buddies know that somebody cared about them.

Over time, more people stepped up in support of these organizations. Among them was Diana, Princess of Wales. In 1987, she visited a London hospital to open the U.K.'s first specialist HIV/AIDS unit.

While photographers snapped away, a smiling Diana reached out and warmly shook the hand of Ivan Cohen, a thirty-two-year-old HIV patient. Ivan asked that his face was not photographed because there was so much judgment associated with the virus at the time. When Diana shook his hand, she wore no gloves and showed no fear. This was at a time when many thought that HIV was spread by touch. With one simple gesture, Diana helped show the world that people with HIV needed kindness and compassion, not suspicion and fear.

Today, people understand that HIV spreads when infected blood or certain bodily fluids enter the body. Now that we know this, the spread can be prevented. While there is still no cure for HIV, medicines allow most people with the virus to live a long and healthy life.

The message of understanding and kindness spread by the pioneering HIV activists made all the difference to people living with the virus and saved many lives.

AN UNCONVENTIONAL DOCTOR

HASSEN BOUCHAKOUR AND DR. PEYO, FRANCE

In a cancer hospital in the French city of Calais, there is one doctor who can always be relied upon to raise a smile on the faces of sick patients. His name is Dr. Peyo and, unlike other medics, he has no stethoscope, thermometer, or white coat.

In fact, he can't even write a prescription. This is because Dr. Peyo is a horse!

Before he began working in the hospital, Peyo and his trainer, Hassen Bouchakour, used to wow the crowds with their impressive **dressage** moves in large arenas. After each show, Peyo would trot to particular people in the crowd and make friends with them. Hassen noticed that his horse had a clever way of choosing people who were sick, sad, or lonely and needed cheering up.

Sensing that Peyo had a unique skill, Hassen spoke to vets and medical experts who agreed that the horse had an unusual ability. Eager to put this gift to good use, Hassen decided to leave the bright lights of the show ring and spend three years preparing Peyo to visit sick and elderly patients. During that time, he gradually introduced Peyo to the unusual sounds, sights, and feel of hospitals and nursing homes.

Great care goes into getting Peyo ready for his visits. His body is gently covered in antiseptic lotion and his mane and tail are tightly braided. When Peyo arrives in the hospital ward for the start of his working day, he stops or raises his leg to show Hassen which room he wants to go into. It's as if he can tell who needs him the most.

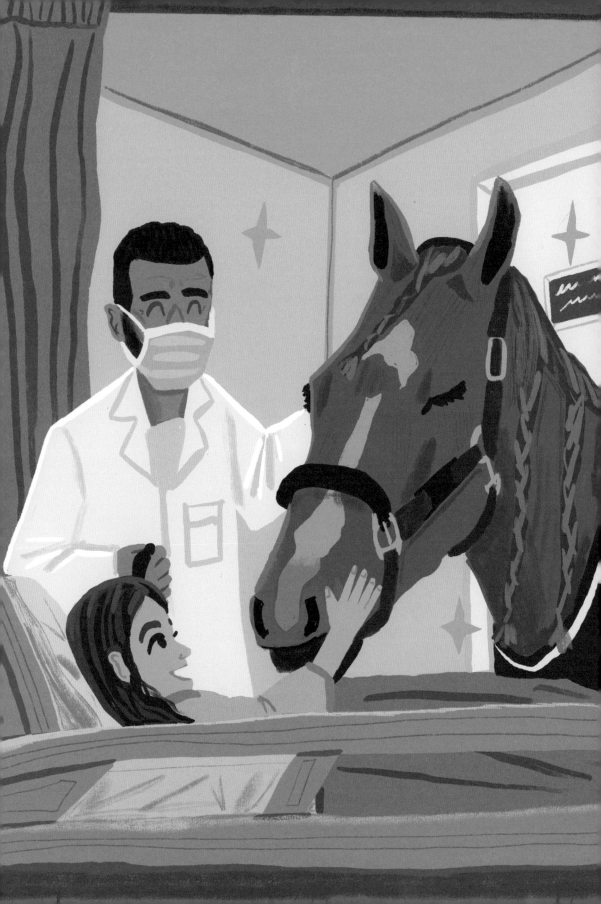

With Hassen's help, Peyo visits patients whose lives are drawing to a close. Hassen watches while Peyo comforts patients with his gentle presence and soft nuzzles, offering them some calmness and love in their final weeks on Earth.

It might sound strange, but it really does work. Patients who spend time with Peyo feel more peaceful and less anxious. Doctors have even found that those who receive visits from Peyo need a lower dose of painkillers!

It's not just the patients who enjoy Peyo's presence. The staff and visitors adore him too because they know that, when things get too tough, they can rely on him to cheer them up.

Since 2016, Dr. Peyo and Hassen have treated over 1,000 patients. For each one, kindness is the most precious medicine of all.

THE SUPPORT OF STRANGERS

SHIRLEY NOLAN, AUSTRALIA

When Anthony Nolan was born in Australia in 1974, doctors diagnosed him with a rare **blood disorder** called Wiskott-Aldrick syndrome. The only hope of a cure was an operation called a **bone marrow transplant**.

Desperate to help her son, Anthony's mom, Shirley, took him halfway around the world, to London. The doctors there agreed to treat Anthony, but they needed to find him a donor whose **stem cells** matched his. The transplant simply wouldn't work without one.

Finding a match was a huge task, a bit like searching for a needle in a haystack. How could they go hunting for stem cells among total strangers?

Shirley sprang into action. She set up the world's first ever **registry** of bone marrow donors. The idea was that volunteers would have their blood tested to see if their stem cells were a match for someone, anyone, in need.

The support from the public was incredible! Over the next five years, Shirley put in endless energy and effort to finding a match for Anthony and others like him.

To her delight, more and more people came forward in the hope that they might be able to help save a life. By 1979, around 30,000 people had registered as possible donors.

Tragically, none of them were a match for Anthony and he passed away that year. Despite her pain and sadness, Shirley worked harder than ever to continue finding donors for others in need. Every bit of data gathered was carefully recorded. Although it had been too late for Anthony, the data might be the exact match for someone else.

In the year that Anthony died, eighty children were on the waiting list for matches. Today, more than a million life-saving stem cell transplants have taken place worldwide. Meanwhile, tens of millions of potential bone marrow donors are registered around the globe.

Shirley later told people that her greatest reward was knowing that her little boy did not die in vain. He certainly didn't. It is because of Anthony and Shirley and the thoughtfulness of complete strangers that millions of lives have been saved.

QUESTIONS

1.

WHY DO YOU THINK PRINCESS DIANA'S KINDNESS TOWARD
IVAN COHEN WAS SO IMPORTANT FOR PEOPLE LIVING
WITH HIV?

2.

CAN YOU THINK OF A TIME WHEN AN ANIMAL HAS HELPED
YOU FEEL HAPPIER, CALMER, OR MORE AT EASE, LIKE
DR. PEYO?

3.

CAN YOU THINK OF THREE WORDS TO DESCRIBE SHIRLEY
NOLAN? WHY DID YOU CHOOSE THESE WORDS?

KINDNESS IN SPORTS

If you've taken part in your school sports day, or watched your favorite team play a game, you've probably seen moments of generosity and goodwill amid the fierce rivalry!

   This tradition of fair play is an important part of being an athlete. It's what makes playing sport such a powerful force for good. It is a way of spreading kindness and understanding between different teams, communities, and even countries, as the stars of our next stories are here to show you . . .

THE OLYMPIC SPIRIT

JESSE OWENS AND LUZ LONG, UNITED STATES AND GERMANY

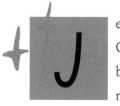

Jesse Owens was the shining star of the 1936 Berlin Olympics in Germany—winning four gold medals and breaking two world records. However, he might not have received one of his medals were it not for an act of kindness from someone completely unexpected.

Our story begins when Jesse lined up for his third and final attempt at qualifying for the long jump finals. To Jesse's frustration, he had messed up his first two attempts (his feet had touched the foul line). He knew that if he fouled again, he would be eliminated from the event. The pressure was on.

As he prepared for his final try, the German long jump champion, Luz Long, walked over and offered some friendly words of advice. He suggested that Jesse should start his run-up further back, so he would take off well before the foul line.

Taking his advice on board, a delighted Jesse qualified for the final. Not only that, he went on to win the gold medal for his country, and to top it off, he also broke the Olympic record!

Luz won the silver medal but was the first to congratulate Jesse with a hug. Afterward, the pair walked out of the cheering stadium arm in arm.

Luz's act of kindness was surprising for two reasons. First, although he was Jesse's main challenger for gold, Luz had put personal and national rivalry aside to help his fellow athlete. Second, the Olympics were being held in Nazi Germany, where there was an atmosphere of intense racism—which was also the case at home in Jesse's country, the United States.

While the world watched on, Luz and Jesse defiantly demonstrated how kindness was a force to combat **prejudice**.

Describing that moment, Jesse later said: "It took a lot of courage for him to befriend me. You can melt down all the medals and cups I have and they wouldn't be a plating on the 24-karat friendship I felt for Luz Long at that moment. Hitler must have gone crazy watching us embrace."

The two athletes remained friends and years later, after Luz had been killed in the war, Jesse visited Luz's son, Kai, in Germany. He celebrated Kai's father with these words: "The only bond worth anything between human beings is their humanness."

A VICTORY FOR KINDNESS

ABEL MUTAI AND IVAN FERNANDEZ ANAYA, KENYA AND SPAIN

As Kenyan long-distance runner Abel Mutai neared the end of his cross-country race, he suddenly slowed down. In a moment of confusion, he thought he'd passed the finish line to take first place, when in fact the line was still 10 yards (30 feet) away.

Abel had been the clear winner of the race, so when Spanish runner Ivan Fernandez Anaya began closing in fast behind him, the crowd held their breath. After a grueling 10 km (6.2 miles) of running, it looked like Abel was about to lose his hard-won victory at the final moment.

But to the crowd's delight, instead of overtaking Abel and claiming glory for himself, Ivan shouted out to him that the race was not over.

When he realized Abel didn't understand Spanish, Ivan caught up with him and guided him to the finish line. Turning around, a relieved and grateful Abel gave his opponent a warm smile and a heartfelt handshake.

When asked why he had chosen to help Abel, rather than take advantage of his mistake, Ivan replied: "My dream is that one day we can have some sort of community life where we push ourselves and help each other to win."

Although Ivan had not come first place, he had undoubtedly won a victory for fair play and kindness.

THE SISTERHOOD OF SPORTSWOMANSHIP

NIKKI HAMBLIN AND ABBEY D'AGOSTINO, NEW ZEALAND AND UNITED STATES

D uring the 2016 Rio Olympics, two runners made headlines for their incredible performance on the track—but not in the way you might imagine.

Nikki Hamblin (New Zealand) and Abbey D'Agostino (U.S.) were competing in the 5,000-meter race when disaster struck: Nikki stumbled and fell. In the chaos that followed, Abbey also took a tumble.

As the rest of the racers charged off into the distance, Abbey struggled to her feet. She helped Nikki do the same, telling her, "Get up, we need to finish this."

Although both were injured and in pain, they gritted their teeth and carried on together. When Abbey fell for a second time, it was Nikki who picked her up and encouraged her to carry on.

Cheered on by the crowds, both athletes eventually managed to complete the race, with Abbey limping in excruciating pain for the last mile. As she crossed the line to loud shouts of support, Nikki met her with a hug.

Although their dreams of Olympic glory had been shattered, they had experienced something extraordinary together.

"It was so special," said Nikki. "Just to celebrate the good that came out of it—that moment together was just unbelievable." Their kindness to one another has been described as one of the most beautiful occasions of the 2016 Olympics.

While the pair left the games without medals, they didn't go home empty handed. Both received the International Olympic Committee's highly prized Fair Play Award in recognition of their sporting kindness.

QUESTIONS

1.

WHAT DO THE ACTIONS OF LUZ LONG, IVAN FERNANDEZ ANAYA, ABBEY D'AGOSTINO, AND NIKKI HAMBLIN HAVE IN COMMON?

2.

CAN YOU THINK OF AN EXAMPLE IN YOUR LIFE WHERE YOU HAVE SHOWN KINDNESS TO SOMEONE, EVEN IF IT MEANT THAT YOU LOST OUT OR DIDN'T DO AS WELL AS YOU EXPECTED TO?

3.

THINK ABOUT ALL SIX ATHLETES. HOW DO YOU THINK THEY FELT AFTER THEIR SPORTING EVENTS WERE OVER?

KINDNESS TOWARD PLANET EARTH

All of our stories so far have been about kindness to people. But surely it's not just humans who deserve human kindness, you might be thinking? And you'd be right!

We live in a vast **ecosystem** where every living thing works together to create a delicate bubble of life. It's a bubble that needs extra care if we want to protect it from popping. While some humans are only just beginning to understand this, others have already taken incredible action.

This chapter will look at ordinary people who have taken big and small steps to care for our precious planet.

BEACHCOMBING FOR PLASTIC

AFROZ SHAH, INDIA

When a young Indian lawyer, Afroz Shah, moved into a seaside apartment in Mumbai he was horrified by the carpet of plastic garbage covering the beautiful beach below.

There was so much of it, you could hardly see the sand! In some places the mounds of waste were more than five feet high. Some of it had been dumped there by people, but most had been washed up by the sea.

Together with his eighty-four-year-old neighbor, Harbansh Mathur, Afroz put on some gloves and began picking up the garbage, one piece at a time.

Lots of people in the neighborhood told Afroz it was a pointless task and that he could never complete it, but still he carried on. Bit by bit, volunteers began to join him—and soon there were lots of them. They included people living in the poorest parts of Mumbai, Bollywood stars, and politicians. Each weekend they gathered up the rotting garbage in the blistering heat, together.

Since 2015, when Afroz and Harbansh started the clean-up, thousands of volunteers have collected millions of pounds of garbage from the waterfront. What was once a seaside dump is now a beach again.

The transformation has been welcomed by wildlife too! In March 2018, volunteers spotted around eighty baby olive ridley turtles waddling toward the sea. This species had not been seen on the beach for over twenty years.

Today, Afroz and his volunteers continue to clean India's beaches, rivers, and mangrove swamps. His work has inspired other beach clean-ups around the world and he hopes that it will motivate many more. "We have more than 7 billion people," he says. "If each one could start, this journey could become marvelous. Can we do it together?"

BATTLING THE BURGER GIANTS

ELLA AND CAITLIN MCEWAN, UNITED KINGDOM

**M**ost families have small plastic toys hiding around the house. Some are played with once and then forgotten about. Many of these toys might come free of charge, inside a chocolate egg or with a meal. I wonder if you have some at home?

Although they aren't big, these kinds of toys create a huge problem for our environment. This is because they take around 500 years to **decompose**.

When Ella and Caitlin McEwan (who were ten and eight) learned about this problem in school, they decided to act. They talked to their parents about what they could do, then decided to start an online petition against plastic toys in fast-food meals.

They wanted two famous fast-food chains in particular—McDonalds and Burger King—to stop handing out the toys with their children's meals. They knew that both companies sold over a billion kids' meals around the world each year, which meant a lot of plastic toys!

After a slow start, their petition went viral. More than half a million people signed to say they agreed with Ella and Caitlin. The girls even went to the McDonalds headquarters in the U.K. They took with them three cartloads containing nearly 2,000 tiny plastic toys. The idea was to show the huge number being handed out every five minutes in the U.K.

Their voices were heard loud and clear. It spurred McDonalds and Burger King into action. Both companies have stopped giving away hard plastic toys with their children's meals in the U.K., Ireland, and France.

Ella and Caitlin were overjoyed by their McHappy ending. Their thoughtfulness for our planet has spurred big conversations and, importantly, big change. They now hope that other big companies will do their part to cut plastic waste and help protect the planet for future generations.

DEFENDING THE CLIMATE IN COURT

ANJ SHARMA, AUSTRALIA

In 2021, eight teenage climate activists and a nun took on the Australian Government. It was a court battle that gripped the world. The group—led by sixteen-year-old Anjali (Anj) Sharma—were trying to stop the expansion of a massive coal mine.

Anj and her friends were horrified that their government was in favor of increasing coal production in Australia. You don't have to be an environmental expert to know that burning coal is the most polluting way of producing energy!

Anj was frightened. Australia had been hit by horrific forest fires and her relatives in India were already suffering from the effects of severe flooding caused by climate change. She knew that time was running out. What's more, she was angry that decision-makers weren't thinking about the impact of their choices on future generations. So, she decided to do something about it!

Along with seven friends and the help of an eighty-six-year-old nun named Sister Brigid Arthur, Anj began a legal case against the Australian environment minister.

The teenagers and their lawyers argued that the minister had a duty to protect younger people against future harm caused by climate change. If the minister allowed the mine extension to go ahead, she would be failing in that duty.

To the teenagers' delight—and the world's amazement—the judge agreed with them.

Sadly, the victory was shortlived. The minister challenged the judge's decision in another court battle and succeeded. The coal mine expansion that Anj and her team had fought hard to stop was given the go-ahead.

Even though this battle was not won, Anj and her team set an important example for all of us to stand up for the planet. Anj continues to fight climate change with all her might. As a caring **world citizen** (see p. 111) she believes she has no choice. It is her duty.

QUESTIONS

1.

HOW HAVE AFROZ SHAH'S ACTIONS IMPACTED BOTH
BEACHES IN INDIA AND THOSE AROUND THE WORLD?

2.

ELLA AND CAITLIN MCEWAN WERE STILL IN ELEMENTARY
SCHOOL WHEN THEY CAMPAIGNED AGAINST SMALL PLASTIC
TOYS. CAN YOU THINK OF A SMALL CHANGE YOU COULD MAKE
THAT COULD HAVE A POSITIVE IMPACT ON OUR WORLD?

3.

WHAT HAVE THESE THREE STORIES TAUGHT YOU ABOUT
BEING KIND TOWARD PLANET EARTH?

KINDNESS TOWARD ANIMALS

Humans and animals have a long and close relationship. Humans are, after all, just another kind of animal! We share the planet with creatures big and small, which means it's often helpful for us to work together.

Have you heard of the clever dolphins who saved swimmers from sharks? What about pet dogs who know when their owner is sad, and try to cheer them up? There are countless examples of animals showing kindness to humans, and every creature, whether it's an elephant or an ant, plays an important role on our planet. We should be kind to them all.

On discovering that some species are struggling for survival, the people in our next stories have stood up to help our furry and feathered friends.

SAVING THE BEARS

SALVIAMO L'ORSO, ITALY

Italy's shy marsican bear has been called one of the most peaceful bears in the world. When it's not hunting for food (roots, fruit, honey, or the occasional small animal), or scratching itself on its favorite trees, it likes to keep itself to itself.

Yet, while humans have nothing to fear from these easygoing creatures, the bears cannot say the same about us! Eager to protect their beehives, orchards, and livestock from raids, people have sometimes resorted to hunting and poisoning the bears.

What's more, the bears have suffered from the destruction of their **habitat** by humans farming more land and building greater numbers of houses and roads. Where there were once hundreds of marsican bears roaming around Italy's Apennine Mountains, there are now around fifty living in the Abruzzo National Park and its surrounding mountains.

But all is not lost, thanks to the kindness of some dedicated nature lovers. In 2012, a group of concerned bear enthusiasts set up a charity called Salviamo l'Orso (Save the Bear).

Volunteers remove stretches of treacherous barbed wire from the mountains, and install light and sound reflectors on busy roads to keep the bears from venturing onto them in the dark. In the spring, they prune abandoned apple and cherry trees so that the bears can enjoy the free fruit later in the year without upsetting anyone.

They also place electric fencing around farmers' orchards, beehives, and livestock. This protects the farmers' crops from the hungry bears and the hungry bears from angry farmers!

Their most difficult task is to create **wildlife corridors**. These corridors are free from human-made obstacles and allow bears to reach nearby national parks safely. Building these wildlife corridors involves planting fruit and nut trees and clearing old paths that run beneath roads for the bears to use.

It's a huge task that will take many long years to bear(!) fruit. But it's something that the volunteers do out of love and respect for these critically endangered bears.

FOSTERING BEARDED VULTURES

ALEX LLOPIS DELL, SPAIN

 **T**he majestic bearded vulture once soared across the mountain ranges of southern Europe, from Spain to the Balkans. But, like the marsican bear in the previous story, their populations were nearly wiped out by hunting, illegal wildlife poisoning, and habitat disturbance.

In fact, the bearded vulture would probably be extinct in Europe by now if it wasn't for the efforts of some determined **conservationists**. One of them in particular, Dr. Alex Llopis Dell, will stop at nothing to save this amazing bird.

Dr. Alex works in a bearded vulture captive breeding center in Catalonia, Spain. Here he helps hatch and raise baby vultures to release into the wild. He is so passionate about helping this struggling species that he has even teamed up with a male vulture to raise chicks.

Alex's vulture partner is called Kajazo. Kajazo was **hand-reared** in a zoo, meaning he was looked after by humans as a young bird and now believes that humans are his species (a process experts call **human imprinting**).

In early autumn each year, Dr. Alex and Kajazo start preparing by building a nest together from sticks and wool. When it's ready, Dr. Alex places a pretend egg in the nest. He and Kajazo then take it in turns to sit on the egg, just as bearded vultures do in the wild.

Dr. Alex sits on the egg for an hour a day, between September and March. Meanwhile, staff at the center artificially **incubate** an actual vulture egg. This egg has been laid by another breeding pair who can't look after their eggs for different reasons, including injury.

When the real egg hatches, Dr. Alex replaces the dummy egg with a fluffy chick!

Usually, Kajazo accepts the chick and begins raising it. He keeps it warm and feeds it with scraps of meat. Once the chick is old enough and in good shape, it is released into the wild.

Alex and Kajazo raise one chick a year, playing a valuable role in reintroducing the species into the wild. Thanks to the efforts of the vulture **conservationists**, over 340 chicks have been released into the wild, meaning bearded vultures can soar over the mountains of Europe once again!

QUESTIONS

1.

IN WHICH DIFFERENT WAYS HAS SALVIAMO L'ORSO WORKED
TO KEEP THE ABRUZZO NATIONAL PARK AND ITS SURROUNDING
MOUNTAINS SAFE FOR BEARS? CAN YOU THINK OF ANY OTHER
EXAMPLES OF PEOPLE DOING AMAZING THINGS TO KEEP
ANIMALS SAFE?

2.

HOW HAS THE KINDNESS OF ALEX LLOPIS DELL HELPED
PREVENT THE EXTINCTION OF BEARDED VULTURES IN
SOUTHERN EUROPE?

3.

CAN YOU THINK OF ANY WAYS YOU CAN SHOW KINDNESS
TO ANIMALS YOU COME ACROSS EACH DAY? WHETHER IT'S
FEEDING WILD BIRDS OR WALKING A PET DOG, EVERY ACT
OF KINDNESS COUNTS.

KIND CUSTOMS

Kindness, like people, comes in colorful variety. The bigger deeds might seem mighty and brave, but the small ones are just as important. Even the tiniest act can create a powerful ripple effect.

In this chapter you will read about entire communities who place simple acts of kindness at the heart of their cultures and customs. Together, they celebrate the fact that we can all do something every day—from making someone smile, to holding the door open for another person. They are small actions that fill our world with kindness.

WALL OF KINDNESS

IRAN

A wall of kindness is a place where people leave donations—on hooks and pegs—for those who need them.

The idea started in Iran in 2015. There, in the city of Mashhad, a kindhearted person left some warm clothes hanging on a wall. Next to it they wrote: "If you don't need it, leave it. If you need it, take it."

The idea inspired others to do the same and soon more people began to leave their offerings on the wall too.

It was not long before the idea spread to other cities around the world, including Luizhou in China, London in the U.K., Cork in Ireland, and Kabul in Afghanistan.

OMOTENASHI

JAPAN

When Japanese soccer fans watch their national team in action, they always stay behind afterward to help stadium workers clean up the garbage.

This is just one of the traditions that stems from the **philosophy** of **omotenashi**. Put simply, omotenashi is the idea that you should treat everyone in the best possible way—with consideration and respect—without expecting anything in return.

The philosophy goes back hundreds of years and has its roots in Japan's traditional tea ceremony. During these ceremonies, the host does everything for the enjoyment of their guests.

These days, you can see omotenashi in action in all parts of Japanese life. If someone loses something in Japan, they are likely to get it back. Even money. If someone is planning construction, it's traditional to give the neighbors gift-wrapped laundry detergent before they start—to wash their clothes if they get covered in construction dust!

Visitors to Japan sometimes comment on how easy it is to slip into the ways of omotenashi. Being treated with consideration naturally makes them become more considerate too. Imagine what might happen if every visitor took the idea home with them!

THE WORLD'S MOST GENEROUS COUNTRY

INDONESIA

I wonder if you can guess which countries are the most generous, or giving, in the world? You might think they would be the richest countries, but you'd be wrong!

One country that topped the world's generosity charts in recent years (either coming in first place or in the top ten) is Indonesia.

According to the World Giving Index (WGI)—which measures how much people around the world give to others—Indonesians are more likely to donate money, help strangers, and volunteer than people in most other countries. Why?

One of the main reasons for this is religion. Indonesia contains the largest Muslim population of all countries in the world. One of Islam's five pillars (key practices) is **zakat**, which invites individuals to donate a certain amount of their money to charities each year.

Another reason is the country's tradition of **gotong royong** (helping each other). Gotong royong is about working together for the community. It encourages an unselfish way of life.

So, when someone builds a house, the neighbors will help them do it. Or when a family hosts a wedding party, the neighborhood will help prepare and serve the food. Members of a community will work together to solve problems, clean public spaces, and look after each other during tough times.

Gotong royong shows that generosity doesn't just mean giving money. We can all be generous with our time and energy, our laughter and thoughts, and, of course, our kindness.

CAFFÈ SOSPESO

NAPLES, ITALY

Have you ever had a stroke of luck, or a surprisingly joyful moment, that has made you want to pass on your happiness to someone else? Even to a total stranger?

In Naples, Italy, many years ago, this desire to pass on happiness started a wonderful tradition called **caffè sospeso**. Caffè sospeso means "suspended coffee" and this is how it works.

If someone has had a good day or simply feels like doing something kind, they can go into a café and pay for two coffees, but only drink one. Someone else who can't afford to buy a coffee can then come in and have the coffee that was already paid for.

Instantly, their day will be that little bit better. Who knows? They might well be inspired to perform an act of kindness themselves.

Caffè sospeso is a simple, anonymous gesture, but a powerful one. It is so powerful, in fact, that from its small beginnings in Naples, it has spread all around the world.

UBUNTU

MANY COUNTRIES IN AFRICA

Africa is a huge continent made up of fifty-four countries. There is a word that is important to people from many of these nations. It is **Ubuntu** and it comes from the southern African phrase: *Umuntu Ngumuntu Ngabantu*, which can be translated as: "I am because you are, you are because we are." In other words, we are all connected, and that connection makes us human.

This means it doesn't matter whether we know someone or not, it is our duty to show them compassion and understanding. When we support and help one other, our own lives become happier and more fulfilled. In other words, one person's success and happiness is everyone's success and happiness.

Among the most famous champions of Ubuntu are Nelson Mandela (see p. 21), South Africa's first Black president, and Desmond Tutu, a Bishop and anti-**apartheid** activist. Both have been awarded the Nobel Peace Prize.

"We think of ourselves far too frequently as just individuals . . . whereas you are connected and what you do affects the whole world," Desmond Tutu said.

Through the work of Nelson Mandela, Desmond Tutu, and many others, Ubuntu thinking was adopted in South Africa. This helped to bring about the end of apartheid (the legal system that separated people by race—see p. 21) peacefully, allowing people in South Africa to work together for a united future.

As Nelson Mandela said, "No one is born hating another person because of the color of his skin, or his background, or his religion. People must learn to hate, and if they can learn to hate, they can be taught to love, for love comes more naturally to the human heart than the opposite."

KINDNESS ON THE UNDERGROUND

LONDON, UNITED KINGDOM

O ne day on the London Underground (the Tube), an artist called Michael Landy watched a passenger help a fellow traveler. The two were complete strangers.

What he saw filled him with so much positivity that he decided to create an art project celebrating everyday kindness on the London Underground. It was called *Acts of Kindness*.

Michael started by inviting passengers and staff to send him stories that they had seen or been part of on the Tube.

He then created posters telling those stories and placed them on trains and platforms.

The tales were many and magical. There was the story of a young boy who let go of his helium balloon and watched helplessly as it floated down the train car. One by one, the smiling passengers batted it back to him.

There was a story of a tearful lady who had received a tissue and a warm smile from the passenger sitting across from her.

Then there was the dusty construction worker who handed his pack of face wipes to a little girl with itchy face-paint on her cheeks. The list went on!

"I wanted to find out what makes us human, and what connects us," Michael explained. "For me the answer is compassion and kindness."

QUESTIONS

1.

WHAT DO ALL THE CUSTOMS IN THIS CHAPTER HAVE IN COMMON?

2.

WHICH OF THESE CUSTOMS IS YOUR FAVORITE AND HOW DOES IT MAKE THE WORLD A BETTER PLACE?

3.

WHAT CUSTOMS COULD YOU INTRODUCE TO YOUR FAMILY, CLASSROOM, OR SCHOOL THAT WOULD HELP TO FILL YOUR WORLD WITH KINDNESS?

CONCLUSION

Remember our alien visitor from the beginning of this book? If they could read these stories—even just some of them—I bet they'd be tempted to hover around and discover more about our planet. That's because each tale shows just how amazing humans can be when they use their kindness superpower.

Whether it's the compassion of the Swiss businessman Henri Dunant (see p. 40), the bravery of the villagers of Le Chambon-sur-Lignon (see p. 15), or the dedication of Hassen Bouchakour and his horse, Dr. Peyo (see p. 58), each story reminds us that we don't have to scratch too far beneath the surface of human nature before a sparkling layer of kindness starts to shine through.

So, if you ever see someone being mean, or hear something that makes you feel sad, just remember: there are more people doing good things and being kind than not. And, if you smiled at someone today, you're one of them! Because it's not just the superhuman acts of heroism that make a difference. Each and every gesture of kindness, from the mighty right down to the minuscule, is precious! Each one is important because it will inspire others to be kind and so help make our world a more caring place.

Above all, remember this: no matter who you are, where you live, or what you do in life, it is always possible to be kind. It might not always be the easiest option—but it will always be the right one.

So, what are we waiting for?

Let's get out there and fill this world with kindness.

IMPORTANT AFTERWORD:
BE KIND TO
YOURSELF!

With so much opportunity to show kindness to others, it can be easy to forget the one person who needs kindness the most: that's you!

You might think that sounds silly. But it's really very sensible. Think about it. How can you help fix things for others if you are in a bad place yourself?

So, remember, look out for yourself as well as others. Kindness is not about saying yes to everything or doing all the work alone. It's about sticking up for people—including yourself.

Take time to notice how you're feeling, then pause for however long you need to reboot and be a kinder you!

KINDNESS
STARS

Some of the world's wisest thinkers have been writing about and discussing the importance of kindness for thousands of years. These are people who thought about life and how best to live it. They concluded that being kind is the key to living happily.

Here are just a few of them and what they had to say.

GAUTAMA BUDDHA

(C. 563–483 BCE)

"In compassion lies the world's true strength."

Gautama Buddha was the first spiritual leader of a religion called Buddhism. Gautama Buddha, also known as Siddharta Gautama, began his teaching around 2,500 years ago.

One of the key things that Buddhists teach is to practice **karuna**, which means compassion. Compassion is a feeling of concern for all living creatures (human and animal) who are suffering and a desire to help them. When you want to help your friend when they aren't feeling well, that's an example of karuna. The Buddha taught that showing compassion to everyone is something we are all capable of.

Another thing that the Buddha taught was the importance of practicing **metta**, or loving kindness. Metta is about showing love and kindness to others *before* they need help. So, doing something kind to make your friend happy would be metta.

As the spiritual leader of Tibet, His Holiness the 14th Dalai Lama, neatly put it: "The key to a happier and more successful world is the growth of compassion. We do not need to become religious, nor do we need to believe in an ideology. All that is necessary is for each of us to develop our good human qualities."

CONFUCIUS

(551–479 BCE)

"What you do not want done to yourself, do not do to others."

Around the same time that Buddhism was spreading through India, one of the most famous philosophers, Confucius (or *K'ung Fu-tzu* in Chinese), was teaching in China.

Although he lived in a time of great disorder and chaos, Confucius believed that humans were naturally good. He was confident that society could get back onto a great path if people worked to behave decently toward each other.

Confucius said that the most important quality a person should have was something called **ren**—which translates as **benevolence**, or being kind! He believed that everyone was born with ren in their hearts, they just needed to nurture it.

Today, the teachings of Confucius can be found in a book called *The Analects*.

ARISTOTLE

(384–322 BCE)

"The good person ought to [love himself], since he will then both benefit himself by acting nobly and aid his fellows."

Aristotle was a respected Greek philosopher who wrote and spoke about science, politics, friendship, happiness, and kindness.

Aristotle said that when it comes to being kind and loving, you must start with yourself. His point was this: how can you understand how to love others and treat them properly, if you can't be kind to yourself?

Aristotle pointed out that there is a healthy self-love and unhealthy self-love. Someone who puts their own needs before those of others, or who takes more than their fair share of things, has an unhealthy and selfish type of self-love. These people aren't able to love others well.

However, a good person—someone who is brave, generous, kind, loyal, and trustworthy—can love themselves in a healthy way. Today we might call this having **self-esteem**—which means having respect for yourself and valuing yourself. Someone with self-esteem is capable of loving others well.

The message: be kind to yourself as well as others!

RUMI

(1207–1273)

Your acts of kindness are iridescent wings of divine love, which linger and continue to uplift others long after your sharing

Rumi (Jalāl ad-Dīn Muhammad Balkhī) was a thirteenth-century poet, writer, and Islamic scholar who lived in Konya, in present-day Turkey.

Rumi taught and wrote about the importance of tolerance, patience, love, compassion, and kindness. One of his most famous poems, above, describes how acts of kindness continue to touch people's lives long after they have taken place (just like we discussed in Chapter One).

Rumi's poems have been widely translated into many of the world's languages. His work is so popular that his words of wisdom can often be found on car bumper stickers and fridge magnets!

JEAN-JACQUES ROUSSEAU
(1712–1778)

"What wisdom can you find that is greater than kindness?"

Jean-Jacques Rousseau was a Swiss philosopher who, like Confucius, believed humans were naturally good. The problem was, they did not always stay that way. This made Rousseau wonder if something could be done to stop people from becoming selfish. He decided that one of the answers was education.

It was important, he said, for adults to teach children by example. "Men, be kind to your fellow-men," he wrote. "This is your first duty, kind to every age and station."

He also warned people that kindness was about much more than handing out money and things to those in need.

"In vain will you open your purse if you do not open your heart along with it . . . You must give your own time, attention, affection, your very self . . . love others and they will love you."

GABRIELA MISTRAL

(1889–1957)

But don't fall prey to the error that only
Great tasks done can be counted
as accomplishments.
There are small acts of service that
are good ones:
Decoratively setting a table,
Putting some books in order,
Combing a little girl's hair.

The Chilean poet, teacher, and diplomat Gabriela Mistral was the first Latin American author to receive the Nobel Prize in Literature. Her real name was Lucila Godoy Alcayaga, but she used the name Gabriela Mistral for her writing.

Throughout Gabriela's life, she bravely spoke up for the rights of disadvantaged groups in society, including the indigenous people of Latin America, women, children, poor people, and many others.

Kindness and compassion were important themes in her writing. In one of her most famous poems, *The Pleasure of Serving* (above), Gabriela makes the point that simple acts of kindness are as important and meaningful as big ones.

ANNE FRANK

(1929–1945)

"If everyone were to give . . . and didn't scrimp on kindly words, there would be much more love and justice in the world!"

Anne Frank was a German girl and Jewish victim of the Holocaust, the persecution of the Jewish population under the Nazis. Anne is famous for writing about her experiences in her diary while she and her family spent two years hiding in a cramped, secret apartment in Amsterdam.

Although Anne suffered and saw terrible things, her faith in the power of human kindness remained strong. She spent a lot of time thinking and writing about this during her time hiding. Her book, *The Diary of a Young Girl*, continues to be read across the world. In her words: "Open your eyes, be fair in your own dealings first! Give whatever there is to give! You can always—always—give something, even if it's a simple act of kindness."

"Give and you shall receive, much more than you ever thought possible. Give and give again. Keep hoping, keep trying, keep giving! People who give will never be poor!'

MAYA ANGELOU

(1928–2014)

"I'm convinced of this: Good done anywhere is good done everywhere."

Maya Angelou was an American author, poet, and **civil rights** activist. Born in 1928, in St. Louis, Missouri, Maya lived through a time of **segregation** and deep-rooted racism in America.

She used writing as a powerful tool to show injustice and speak up about what would make the world a fairer, better, and more equal place for everyone to live. Throughout her life, Maya wrote poetry, stories, and essays based on her experiences. Her wise messages of kindness, courage, and hope continue to inspire people all over the world today.

Here are just a few of her thoughts on kindness:

"Just do right . . . make it a better world. Just where you are. And it can be better. And it must be better. But it is up to us."

"For a change, start by speaking to people rather than walking by them like they're stones that don't matter. As long as you're breathing, it's never too late to do some good."

MARTHA NUSSBAUM

(1947–PRESENT)

"Knowledge is no guarantee of good behavior, but ignorance is a virtual guarantee of bad behavior."

Martha Nussbaum is one of the most well-known and respected philosophers living today. She believes that we should show concern and respect for all human beings, and that we should extend this concern and respect to animals too.

Martha's belief is based on the idea that we are not just citizens of our own countries—but of the entire world.

As "**world citizens**" we should be committed to caring about and helping the millions who suffer from tragedies like war, malnutrition, and disease—in all countries, not just our own.

The trouble is, she says, that in many countries—including her own country, the United States—most people's concern for others stops at the national boundary (the border).

Like Jean-Jacques Rousseau, she believes that education is key to making people's concern stretch further and making our world a better place.

Through the right kind of teaching, she believes, people can learn to become compassionate world citizens.

GLOSSARY

ACHONDROPLASIA
A genetic condition that causes a person to have shorter-than-average limbs.

ACTIVIST
A person who campaigns for change, usually on political or social issues.

AFRICAN NATIONAL CONGRESS (ANC)
A South African political party that opposed apartheid.

AFRIKAANS
A language spoken in several African countries, including South Africa.

APARTHEID
From the Afrikaans word for "apartness." A system of laws under which Black and non-white South African people were denied the same rights as white South Africans.

BENEVOLENCE
The quality of being selflessly kind.

BLOG
An online journal, diary, or newsfeed, sometimes about a person's life, hobbies, or interests.

BLOOD DISORDER
A condition that means a person's blood is unable to do the things it normally does.

BONE MARROW
A substance, full of blood vessels, found in the center of bones.

BONE MARROW TRANSPLANT
When unhealthy bone marrow is removed from a person's body and replaced by healthy bone marrow from a donor.

CAFFÈ SOSPESO
Italian for "suspended coffee." Ordering one coffee but paying for two—the second coffee is given to the next customer as a gift.

CIVIL RIGHTS
The promise of equal social and political rights (such as the right to vote or marry) for all people in a society.

CIVIL WAR
A war that takes place between two or more groups within the same country or region.

CIVILIAN
A person who is not in the armed forces and does not fight during times of war.

COMPASSION
A feeling of sympathy for someone in need and the desire to help them.

THE CONFEDERACY
One side in the American Civil War, made up of states that were in favor of slavery.

CONSERVATIONIST
Someone who studies and looks after endangered species to protect them from extinction.

CULTURE
The customs and traditions of a particular group of people.

CUSTOM
A belief or way of behaving that has been around for a long time.

DECOMPOSE
When something breaks down over time.

DICTATOR
A ruler who has absolute power over a country and its people.

DRESSAGE
A type of horse-riding competition in which the horse and rider perform for judges, almost like a dance.

ELECTION
The process of casting votes to decide who should hold an official position of power.

ECOSYSTEM
A group of plants, animals, and their environment, all of which depend on each other.

FIVE PILLARS OF ISLAM
The five key practices of the religion of Islam, which a Muslim should try to carry out throughout their lifetime.

GENDER
How a person identifies themselves: as a boy, a girl, or non-binary.

GENETIC CONDITION
A difference in a person's genes that can alter growth or health.

GOTONG ROYONG
The Indonesian tradition of helping others and the community.

HABITAT
The natural home of a plant or animal.

HAND-REARED
An animal that has been raised
by humans in captivity.

HORMONE
One of the chemicals in the body
that control how you develop
and grow.

HULL
The main body of a ship or boat.

HUMAN IMPRINTING
When an animal is raised by humans
from a young age, and believes
humans are its species.

HUMANITARIAN
A person who works to make
life better for others.

INCLUSIVE
Designed to include and be
fair to everybody, regardless of
race, gender, physical ability, or
any other difference between
people.

INCUBATE
When egg-laying animals (such as
birds) sit on their eggs to keep
them warm before they hatch.

KARUNA
Compassion.

LIBELOUS
When something written or printed
contains a false statement about a
person that might cause them to
be treated badly.

LIBERTY
Freedom.

LITTLE PERSON
Someone who is shorter than
average due to a genetic condition
(such as achondroplasia).

METTA
The Buddhist practice of
"loving kindness."

MINORITY
Less than half of the people
in a society.

NEUROTRANSMITTER
One of many chemicals that carry
messages between different parts of
the body, telling them what to do.

NEUTRAL
Supporting no side in a conflict.

NON-BINARY
A person who does not identify as
a boy or a girl. They may be a little
of both, neither, or somewhere
in between.

OMOTENASHI
The belief that you should treat
everyone with consideration and
respect without expecting a reward.

OPTIMIST
A person who is hopeful for the
best possible future.

PERSECUTED; PERSECUTION
When a person or group of
people is badly treated because
of a "difference" between them
and another group, such as their
ethnicity or religion.

PHILOSOPHY
A custom or belief about the way the
world works and how to act toward
the world and other people.

PREJUDICE
When people judge, hate, or
treat others badly because they
are different.

RADIATION
A type of energy that travels very
quickly in waves or particles.

REGISTRY
A list of people who share something
in common, such as the willingness
to donate their bone marrow to a
person in need.

REN
In the Chinese philosophy
of Confucianism, the quality
of being kind.

SELF-ESTEEM
Belief in your own worth and
abilities as a human being.

SEXUALITY
Describes what gender or genders
(if any) a person is attracted to.

SOCIETY
A group of people who live and
work together.

SOLIDARITY
Support of, and agreement with,
a group of people.

SPECIES
A group of animals or plants that
are similar in various ways and can
reproduce with each other.

STEM CELL
A type of cell in our bodies that
can create other cells.

TAIL GUNNER
The person on board a military
aircraft who operates a gun to
defend it from attacks from behind.

TRANS
Used to describe a person whose gender identity is not determined by society's expectations or the body they were born in.

TREASON
When a person betrays their country.

TSUNAMI
A huge and very destructive wave, usually caused by an earthquake under the ocean.

UBUNTU
From the southern African phrase "*Umuntu ngumuntu ngabantu*," meaning "I am because you are, you are because we are," or that all people are connected and should treat each other with compassion and understanding.

UNDERGROUND RAILROAD
A secret network of routes, places, and people used by enslaved people in the South of the United States to escape to freedom in the North.

THE UNION
One side in the American Civil War, which wanted to bring an end to slavery.

WILDLIFE CORRIDOR
A feature in the natural landscape, such as a hedgerow or group of trees, that allows animals to move safely between habitats separated by human-made obstacles.

WISKOTT-ALDRICH SYNDROME
A genetic condition that affects the immune system and bone marrow.

WORLD CITIZEN
A person who lives on Planet Earth. Everybody is a world citizen, including you!

WORLD WAR II
A war that took place between 1939 and 1945, involving many countries.

ZAKAT
The third of the Five Pillars of Islam, encouraging Muslims to give money to charities and good causes.

REFERENCES

BOOKS

Aurelius, Marcus. *The Meditations.*
New York, NY: 2002.

Born This Way Foundation (au.), Lady
Gaga (intro.). *Channel Kindness: Stories of
Kindness and Community.* London: 2020.

Bregman, Rutger. *Humankind: A Hopeful
History.* London: 2019.

Burke, Sinéad (au.), and Byrne, Natalie
(illust.). *Break The Mould: How to Take
Your Place in the World.* London: 2020.

Frank, Anne. *Anne Frank: The Collected
Works.* London: 2019.

Frank, Anne. *The Diary of a Young Girl.*
London: 2007.

Hain, Peter. *Ad & Wal: Values, Duty,
Sacrifice in Apartheid South Africa.*
London: 2014.

Honderich, Ted (ed.). *The Oxford
Companion to Philosophy.* Oxford: 1995.

Jawando, Danielle. *Maya Angelou (Little
Guides to Great Lives).* London: 2019.

Jazynka, Kitson. *DK Life Stories: Harriet
Tubman.* London: 2019.

Moorehead, Carole. *Village of Secrets:
Defying the Nazis in Vichy France.*
London: 2015.

Ngomane, Mungi. *Everyday Ubuntu:
Living Better Together, The African Way.*
London: 2019.

The School of Life. *Big Ideas for Curious
Minds: An Introduction to Philosophy.*
London: 2018.

WEBSITES

art.tfl.gov.uk/projects/acts-of-kindness

kindnessuk.com/global_research.php

mava-foundation.org

www.annefrank.org

www.anthonynolan.org

www.health.harvard.edu/blog/the-heart-and-
science-of-kindness-2019041816447

www.randomactsofkindness.org/the-science-
of-kindness

www.redcross.org.uk/about-us/our-history/
the-beginning-of-the-red-cross

www.salviamolorso.it

www.theschooloflife.com

www.titanicinquiry.org

PODCASTS AND AUDIO

Bellissimo, Sarina. "Sinéad Burke –
'Break The Mould'," *The Bellissimo Files.*
20 October 2020.

Burke, Sinéad, and Lemonada Media.
As Me with Sinéad. 2019–21.

Davis, Daryl. "Why I, as a Black Man, Attend
KKK rallies." TEDxNaperville,
8 December 2017.

Hammond, Claudia. *The Anatomy of Kindness.*
BBC Radio 4, 30 March 2022.

Marcus, Eric. "Magnus Hirschfeld,"
*Making Gay History: LGBTQ Oral Histories
from the Archive.* 25 October 2018.

Trocmé, Magda (interviewee), and
Lewin, Rhoda G. (interviewer).
*Oral history interview with Magda
Trocme.* United States Holocaust
Memorial Council, 2 October 1984.

INDEX